Walk Powerful At Zero

WOMEN' GROUP STUDY ON

WALKING POWERFUL WITH GOD

Volume One

COACH ANNA MCCOY

CONTENTS

Walk Powerful with God: A Journey to ZERO, the Most Powerful Number for Kingdom Living

A Message from the Chief Encouragement Officer, Coach Anna McCoy, Founder of Woman Act Now, the organization and the author of the book, Woman Act Now: Learn, Launch and Live Your Dream

Galatians 2:20— "I am crucified with Christ; nevertheless I live; yet not I, but Christ lives in me: and the life which I now live in the flesh I live by the faith of the Son of God, who loved me, and gave himself for me." For nothing is impossible with God. "Blessed is she who has believed that what the Lord has said to her will be accomplished!" I am convinced that nothing is impossible for God to do in your life. Not only will He do what He says but if you believe what the Lord speaks to you, YOU will accomplish it.

Woman Act Now was conceived out of my passion for walking with women; to teach and equip them to accomplish their Kingdom mandates and life assignment. Woman Act Now is a global movement promoting a culture of honor amongst women to encourage, empower and equip the women of the world to dream bigger, believe in themselves, execute on their ideas and connect with like-minded women to achieve what matters most.

As the founder of this organization, I assure you that I am a woman surrendered to the mantle of releasing women to walk in the power within them. The power I refer to is the surrendered and submitted life I have chosen to live... yielded, aligned, renewed, obedient and radical for God.

Woman Act Now is a call to arms for women to rise to spiritual maturity, not external battle, and walk confidently and persuaded with God. We speak the language of the King; we pursue the marker of ZERO as we decrease and He increases in us; we WomanThink.

We are Power Agents yielded to connect-working with our sisters three-by-three, house by house as we surrender to the power of God in our lives to achieve the dreams, visions, ideas, concepts and strategies to change lives, families, cities and nations. Together we pursue the unquenchable thirst for hope, mobilizing women and offering relevant tools for effective living as transparent and authentic women who walk powerful in every area of our lives.

This is designed as a guide to help women gather together to dialogue about what can be learned as we support each other in our spiritual growth. We are on the journey together and we desire that you, along with at least two of your friends, take a moment to share these treasures with one another.

The Guide

This guide will help you commit to walking with God this year and to experience complete surrender to the purposes of God. It is meant to be shared amongst women, so grab two friends and read it together. Discuss and dialogue on how these principles will impact your growth. We will share scripture with you to meditate upon and questions to ponder.

LESSON ONE
WALK POWERFUL IN SPIRIT

This lesson is to help you understand how to walk powerful in Spirit by choosing to give yourself away to God completely and be a ZERO. To be a zero is to accept yourself as nothing; to yield, to decrease, to surrender, while positioning yourself to experience the ever present presence of God. Can you imagine withholding absolutely nothing of yourself so that you can be used by God to experience supernatural strength, constant provision, manifested glory and love overflowing? Are you ready for this kind of life where peace of mind is a daily occurrence no matter the circumstance, unlimited favor is the norm, and lack is a thing of the past because you walk with the all wise, all knowing God?

In order to live this kind of life that keeps you S.O.A.R.ing you must become surrendered, obedient and radical in your walk with God. We have identified God as our source, His son Jesus as our example and the Holy Spirit as our guide. As we surrender to the power of the source (God) we will experience the manifested glory of God in our lives, we will see our dreams achieved, our relationships healthier, our neighbors healed and our children maturing in Spirit.

The Power Of Zero

The power of zero is a principle to help individuals decrease and allow the Holy Spirit to increase in their life. On a scale of zero to ten, ZERO is the marker for decrease, therefore becoming the most powerful number for Kingdom living.

The world encourages you to be number one at all cost, regardless of who you may destroy in the process, but to be the best in God you must give up everything until you only have your consciousness left and then place that consciousness at the feet of Jesus. What does this mean? To place your consciousness at the feet of Jesus is to humbly submit to His point of view on every matter. Simply, not my will but the Father's will, be done. The power of zero demands that we yield to God's use expecting nothing in return. Choose to be a zero, a flat-liner; to be completely filled and confidently assured and persuaded that your nothingness allows the greater One to emerge from within you.

Become A Power Agent

First, we must understand what power we are connecting into to become powerful to overflowing. We are connected to God who is all wise and all knowing. We are lamps; He is the source who gives us light. We are to be a light and power source to others. Power connectors are a source that is committed to helping women move forward to achieve their destiny. Woman Act Now is a power receptacle for women to plug into to be powered up. Without the acknowledgment of God and Christ-centeredness, we are powerless to give power to others.

Power is energy. God is pure energy and to have the kind of energy that empowers others we must have pure motives.

How To Power Up Others

A power agent is a woman who practices giving power by using these power up principles in her daily life.

Honor - She will give weight to her actions; respect and decrease at the appropriate times. She is no respecter of persons but values, honors and respects others.

Time - Time is value and what you value you give your time. This demonstrates how much worth you give a person, or thing in your life.

Presence – Practice being fully present in the moment, with others, as well as in your personal commitments to self.

Attitude of Love and Gratitude – Love is to contend for

the highest good to be manifested in the present moment. Choose to be grateful for your opportunities and the presence of others in your life. When you acknowledge a person as the gift that they are you will experience the value of that gift.

Retreat to Replenish – Know when you must pull back to recharge with God or disconnect from others or things before you become powerless.

Individual or Group Study

Meet For A Power Hour Group Study: Invite two other friends to discuss this guide and empower each other as you review this lesson.

Scripture: Galatians 2:20 I am crucified with Christ; nevertheless I live; yet not I, but Christ lives in me: and the life which I now live in the flesh I live by the faith of the Son of God, who loved me, and gave himself for me.

1.	What does the Power of Zero mean to you and your ability to walk powerful in Spirit?

2.	Think about and discuss the relationship of the power of zero and being crucified with Christ; nevertheless, I live...how do they relate?

3.	What are the signs that indicate that you have died to self and that you are living by faith?

4.	How does your ego relate to being a ZERO for God and can they co-exist?

5.	How will you decrease to ZERO so that the greater One may emerge from within?

6.	In what aspect of your life do you need to begin to become a zero right now? Marriage, Business, Children,

Health, Finances?

7.   What will you do specifically to become a zero in this regard?

Reflect: Each person takes a minute to reflect on what they have learned or experienced and what they will walk away with from the Power Hour.

Prayer: Father, help me to understand how to decrease and become a ZERO so that you may live within me and use me to accomplish your highest good. Father, your son Jesus loved me enough to give Himself for me and I want to give myself to you to be used to do your will and finish the work you have created me to do. I need your help to die to self and to live by the faith of the Son of God. I decrease today so that you may work a greater work in me so that I may be used for your glory.

Memorize Wan Covenant: This covenant is an agreement between a woman and her word, which holds her accountable for her own success. With this joint effort of others, she will achieve it. Embrace these words, live them and act on them. Become all that you are meant to be.

 Be conscious – I make conscious decisions in my now that positively affect my future now.

Pray for each other's walk away commitment then disperse to reconvene at the agreed time for the next lesson.

Coach Anna McCoy

LESSON TWO
WALK POWERFUL IN VISION

Proverbs 29:18 "Where there is no vision the people perish: but he that keeps the law, happy is he."

Our theme in lesson two is to Walk Powerful in Vision. According to the scripture above, where vision is lacking, the people are headed for destruction. Why is vision such an important component in living powerful?

In 1 Corinthians 4:20, we see that the Kingdom of our God is not in word but in power. As women surrendered to the power of Zero we must demonstrate the power of God in our lives. This lesson will teach you how to hear God, observe what He says and to do what He gives you the vision to achieve.

What Is Vision?

Webster's dictionary defines vision as the ability to think about the future before it happens. It is the ability to think about the future with imagination and wisdom.

Vision is an experience of seeing something in the mind or in a dream or trance.

Vision is the ability to see further than the natural eye can look.

Vision is vivid faith – faith in pictures.

Vision determines destiny; it is the key to the future. It is hope for the future. Jeremiah 29:11.

Vision is what motivates you – when everyone gives up on the project it is what fuels your passion and gives you the grace to be persistent. It is our view of the future as inspired by God.

Let us take a look at Habakkuk 2:1 "I will stand upon my watch, and set me upon the tower, and will watch to see what he will say unto me, and what I shall answer when I am reproved."

It is interesting to me how the Prophet was standing to watch, to see what will be said. Look at the words again, watch, see and hear. When you watch you see, but what you see is that which is shown to you, not that which you hear. So when the Prophet says he will see that which will be said, it means that when the Lord speaks, what He says forms pictures in our mind and whatever picture we can see when He speaks is what we can achieve.

In Deuteronomy 28:1, "And it shall come to pass, if thou shalt hearken diligently unto the voice of the Lord thy God, to observe and to do all his commandments which I command thee this day, that the Lord thy God will set thee on high above all nations of the earth."

Al Hollingsworth, Coach Anna's mentor teaches these three points, hear it, see it, do it now from Deuteronomy 28:1 to equip us to walk powerful in vision.

Hear it–you must hearken diligently to the voice of God

See it–see his Word in pictures to more closely observe what He says

Do it–You must listen with an intent to obey what you see He says and do it now.

Improving your vision requires painstaking effort (diligence) to pursue the pictures of God's spoken word in your life. Decreasing to zero allows us to tap into the ever-present presence of the all-knowing and all-wise God who will show, teach and tell us what to do.

Individual or Group Study

Meet For A Power Hour Group Study: Invite two other friends to discuss this guide and empower each other as you review this lesson.

1.   Greet each other, 'you are loved and appreciated' and quickly review last study and take turns as you each report on how you fared walking as zero in your specific life endeavors.

2.   Study Habakkuk 2:1 and Deuteronomy 28:1, and relate it to Vision, Power and Walking as Zero.

3.   How does the scripture on seeing what you hear

come alive to you?

4.   What does it mean to hear diligently? How does this move into observing?

5.   What is Vision to you specifically? What are you working on that you are sure is God's Vision for your life in this year?

6.   How will you convert what you heard and have seen to something you do? What specific steps do you need to take?

7.   What are you walking away with? Have you been able to own the principle of Walking Powerful in Vision?

Reflect: Each person takes a minute to reflect on what they have learned or experienced and what they will walk away with from the Power Hour.

Memorize Wan Covenant: This covenant is an agreement between a woman and her word, which holds her accountable for her own success. With this joint effort of others, she will achieve it. Embrace these words, live them and act on them. Become all that you are meant to be.

Value education – I value education and sharpen my saw by exploring and learning about people, places, or events that expand my view of the world.

Pray for each other's walk away commitment and disperse to reconvene at the agreed time for the next lesson.

A Message from the Chief Encouragement Officer, Coach   Anna McCoy

Welcome to the third and fourth lessons of the Woman Act Now Journey to Zero. It is most effective in group study, we encourage you to reconvene with your Power Agents or form a new Power Center of three or more women to experience the journey together.

This study will teach you how to Walk Powerful to Persist and Walk Powerful in Being. Zero living requires that you know your identity; you understand how to persist, remain with God and overcome the need for comparisons in your life. Zero living is allowing yourself to engraft the Spirit of God into your being and to consider God's perspective on every matter. It is using the marker of zero to turn down the dial of your personality, desires, emotions and actions to hear, obey and do readily what God says to you to do now..

Coach Anna McCoy

LESSON THREE
WALK POWERFUL TO PERSIST

According to Webster's definition, the word persist means to continue despite difficulties, opposition or discouragement. A common view of persistence in one's life is to stick in there, do whatever is necessary to get what you want or to continue in the fight or finish a course of action. Are you ready to change the way you see the power to persist to do it your way instead of persisting to remain in God so that you may experience the reward of (fill this gap with whatever you desire)? it will be done for you!

Interestingly, the use of words evolve or change according to the times and circumstances in which a word is used. Let's consider the Hebrew meaning of persist which means to abide, remain, continue, or stay. Notice the difference between the emphasis in Webster's current definition and the origins of the word persist in Hebrew. Webster keeps us looking outward to accomplish something as if there is something out there that doesn't want us to have this thing we desire. The Hebrew origins suggest that we are a part of something and we must remain, stay, continue and abide in it.

Our greatest challenge living the Zero life is to remain in God. To remain is to decrease; it is complete surrender for His will to be done. Every moment, hour, or day we are faced with thinking we must solve every problem, that we have the option to abandon righteousness when it is convenient to seek our own way or simply operate in our own power. Walking powerful to persist demands that we no longer press against the grain but rather abide in the vine, stay connected, stay the course, ask God for the things we want and expect it will be done for us because we have persisted to abide in Him rather than persist to fight an enemy, an obstacle, an opposition or to overcome!

John 15:5-8 reads I am the vine; you are the branches. If you remain in me and I in you, you will bear much fruit; apart from me, you can do nothing. 6. If you do not remain in me, you are like a branch that is thrown away and withers; such branches are picked up, thrown into the fire and burned. 7. If you remain in me and my words remain in you, ask whatever you wish, and it will be done for you. 8. This is to my Father's glory, that you bear much fruit, showing yourselves to be my disciples.

There are several lessons to be discovered in this scripture.

1. God is established as the source of life (I am the vine.)

2. We are established as being connected to the source. (Branches connected to the vine.)

3. The purpose of the branch is established. (To produce or bear much fruit, the seed will produce after its kind.)

4. The consequence of disconnection from the Vine. (Nothing will be accomplished.)

5. Law of the power to persist. (If you remain in me and my words remain in you.)

6. The reward of abiding, remaining, staying and continuing in God. (Ask whatever you wish and it will be done for you.)

7. The glory of the Vine–The branches. (You will be productive and fruitful.)

Abiding in God is our answer; His anointing teaches us about all things. Our English language has eroded the power of the word persist and made it something that we can stop when we have grown tired, something we can cease when it is no longer convenient. Without the power of true persistence (abiding in the Vine), we would cease to exist with God, die spiritually, discontinue in truth, quit on our divine destiny, stop pursuing faithfulness and depart from the Way, the Truth and the eternal life of God. We can do nothing without Him but we can do everything remaining in Him.

Individual or Group Study

Meet For A Power Hour Group Study: Invite two other friends to discuss this guide and empower each other as you review this lesson.

Scripture: 1 John 3:9 No one who is born of God will continue to sin because God's seed remains in him; he cannot go on sinning because he has been born of God.

Reflections:

1.   Think about these words, stay, continue, remain and abide, what do they mean to you?

2.   How has your understanding of persistence changed as a result of this study?

3.   How have you persisted to get the things you want in life rather than persisting in God to allow Him to guide you to what He wants for you?

4.   How does persisting equate to Zero living?

5.   Think of a couple of areas in your life that you want to persist to remain in God when you have felt it necessary to do it your own way?

Prayer:

Father, help us to know how to abide in the vine, trust you for the answers that only you can give when we are faced with opposition, challenges or discouragement. I know that as I abide and choose you as my refuge that you will make my way perfect.

I choose to remain in the Vine so that I may be productive for you and experience the wonders of (fill this gap with whatever you desire) and it will be done for me.

Memorize Wan Covenant: This covenant is an agreement between a woman and her word, which holds her accountable for her success. With this joint effort of others, she will achieve it. Embrace these words, live them and act on them. Become all that you are meant to be.

Think Creatively: I commit my time and my mind to thinking creatively, envisioning my future and taking actions on my dreams.

Coach Anna McCoy

LESSON FOUR
WALK POWERFUL IN BEING

Up to a point, a man's life is shaped by environment, heredity, movements and changes in the world around him. Then there comes a time when it lies within his grasp to shape the clay of his life into the sort of thing he wishes to be.

Only the weak blame parents, their race, their times, lack of good fortune, or the quirks of fate. Everyone has it within his power to say, 'This I am today; that I will be tomorrow.'" ~Louis L'Amour

To walk powerful in being I must know my origin; who am I? John 1:3 reads, through him all things were made; without him nothing was made that has been made. To answer the question, "Who am I?" We must ask this question of ourselves and God, where did I exist before I came into being? Being is existence, presence, and life (to be alive). According to the Hebrew translation of hayah (being), the word being means to exist, to be (am), to abide, remain or continue.

Exodus 3:14 states, "And God said unto Moses, I AM THAT I AM; and he said, thus shall thou say unto the children of Israel, I AM hath sent me unto you."

The word AM is being, to be, remain (past or yesterday), exist (present, today) and continue (future, forevermore). Genesis 2:7 the LORD God formed the man from the dust of the ground and breathed into his nostrils the breath of life and the man became a living being (a living AM). I know you might think this is a bit too much to consider yourself "I AM THAT I AM" but I encourage you to consider that you are an "I AM" not "The I AM", and you are more like the "I AM" than you will dare to believe.

The battle for your infinite greatness is locked within your perception of the "I AM" in you.

First, let's revisit mankind's origin. Where did mankind exist before man came to be? Mankind, including you, existed in the thought of God and came to be from a word spoken, Genesis 1:26, Then God said, let us make man in our image, after our likeness... This is our originality, we are made in the image and likeness of God (identity), and in Exodus 3:14 God describes himself as "I AM." The word "AM" can be inserted at the end of Genesis 2:7, and man became a living AM (in the likeness of God). Do not be afraid to be a living AM, should you choose to believe this teaching today you will discover the truth of the "I AM" hidden in you before you were ever knitted together in your mother's womb. No one has the ability to create your "I AM." This journey is about getting to zero and discovering the great "I AM" in you and when you make that discovery you will choose to love yourself and agree with the "I AM that I AM" in you. This is the beckoning we hear, the cry of who am I will be answered by the "I AM."

Reflect the "I Am"

The "I AM" in you will only be strengthened by your knowing the true attributes and character of God. When we believe and demonstrate the knowing of the "I AM's" power within us we will be like that which is mentioned in 2 Corinthians 3:18.

And we, who with unveiled faces all reflect the Lord's glory, are being transformed into his likeness with ever-increasing glory, which comes from the Lord, who is the Spirit. This is the reflection of the "I AM's" power at work in us and through us when we walk powerful in being. If it exists in the "I AM" then the potential of that existence can manifest through mankind or within you. These statements represent "I AM that I am!"

I AM your healer means I am healed
I AM your provider means I am provided for
I AM righteousness means I am righteous

I AM a forgiver means I am forgiven
I AM wisdom means I am wise
I AM just means I am justified
I AM good means I am good
I AM faithful means I am faithful
I AM truth means I am truthful

Creative Law Of "I Am"

Walking powerful in being is owning your "I AM." The only person who can speak words of "I AM" to you is you! People only repeat what they think you are with statements such as, "she is..." or "you are..." The creative law of "I AM" says I alone have the power to speak who I desire to be. When I don't know myself others will define who I am. I have the ability to align my "I AM" decrees with God's image of me.

Meet For A Power Hour Group Study: Invite two other friends to discuss this guide and empower each other as you review this lesson.

Individual or Group Exercise

You are encouraged as a part of this lesson to use the Creative Law of "I AM" by writing out your ABC's of your "I AM." Instructions: On a sheet of paper write the alphabets A-Z. For each alphabet identify an "I AM" that you think will be the most accurate likeness of God in you. For example, write out I AM Able, I AM Bold, I AM Character-centered, I AM Disciplined, I AM Excellent... Once you have written your ABC's take a moment to share them with your Power Agents. Print the "I AMs and repeat them three times a day as affirmations until you have memorized them and engrafted them in your heart. Give yourself twenty-one days of practicing your "I AMs" and you will experience a change in your thoughts, actions, and habits. Also, share this exercise with your children and family and help them identify their ABC's of "I AM."

The Big C: The Enemy Of Walking Powerful In Being

The Big "C" is comparison; it is the enemy of being. Genesis 3:5 "For God doth know that in the day ye eat thereof, then your eyes shall be opened, and ye shall be as gods, knowing good and evil." Pay close attention to what was spoken to Eve, "ye shall be as gods", this is the comparison to something else other than the "I AM" in her. The minute you begin to consider comparing yourself to others rather than remaining in God you will be distracted from believing you are God's creation, assignment, and perfection. Trust Him to complete you.

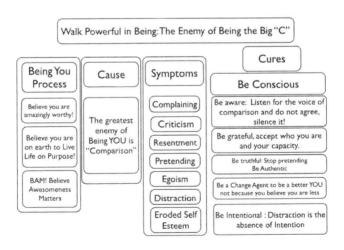

Reflections

1.   How do you identify with the "I AM" in you?

2.   In what areas might you be guilty of comparing yourself to others?

3.   How will you master being more like God?

4.   Can you think of any situation you allowed comparisons to change who you really are?

5.   What consequences have you faced in your life because you chose not to be like God and demonstrate His character and attributes?

Prayer

Father, help us to be more like you. You have made us in your image and your likeness. You want us to be like you, to embody your attributes and your character. Empower us with an understanding of the creative law of "I AM" that we may know you within ourselves as we pursue to be more like you daily.

Teach me how to compare to your likeness and not others so that I may exist to serve you and continue in your Way. In Jesus name, Amen.

Memorize WAN Covenant: This covenant is an agreement between a woman and her word, which holds her accountable for her own success. With this joint effort of others, she will achieve it. Embrace these words, live them and act on them. Become all that you are meant to be.

Master Education: I am an executor of my ideas and I master closing the gap between my thoughts and my actions.

A Message from the Chief Encouragement Officer, Coach Anna McCoy

Welcome to the fifth and sixth lessons of the Woman Act Now Journey to Zero. Convene with your Power Agents or form a new Power Center of three or more women to experience this journey together.

This study will teach you how to recognize the author of your nature, to identify the voices you give attention to and empower you to walk naked (transparently) and unashamed (confident assurance) with God's nature as your guide. You will be encouraged to renew your mind by the Word of God which is the voice of God.

LESSON FIVE
WALK POWERFUL NAKED & UNASHAMED

After Adam and Eve sinned in the Garden of Eden, God confronted Adam with two important questions: "Where art thou?" and "Who told you that you were naked?" (Gen. 3:11, NKJV) He was really asking Adam, "Why have you removed yourself from my presence?" and "Who have you been listening to—other than Me?"

We learned in lesson four, about the big "C" (comparison) and God wanted Adam to realize that he had allowed something other than God's living word to influence him—and as a result, something other than God's nature had entered his heart.

Let's back up for just a moment to revisit the statement "they were naked and unashamed." This statement was made about the state of mind or condition of Adam and Eve when they became one with each other. The word naked is used to refer to their transparency with God and each other, their connectedness, their clarity of assignment of who they were. To be unashamed in this sense was that they were not confused, confounded or troubled but had confident hope in God.

Let's return to the questions, asked of Adam, "Where are you? and "Who told you that you were naked?" It is important to establish that nakedness is also associated with removing the mantle; to be shrewd, crafty or take crafty counsel. God needed no answer but these questions can teach us an important principle: Whatever you give your attention to determines the nature that lives in and rules you. Eve gave her attention to the serpent by opening the gates of her hearing, her sight, and her taste. She allowed the words of the enemy to entice and deceive her to act out of his nature—one characterized by pride, lust, and disobedience. This act opened the passions of their minds to envy, pride, and desire, all of which manifested in the eye.

The word mantle means thick coverlet; it means to lean, to lay, rest, support, uphold, lean upon, to sustain, to refresh and revive. It is derived from the Hebrew root word camak which means to approach, to be connected, and to be near. God wanted to know where the mantle was that had been placed on Adam, and who was the cause of its removal.

The Bible states that Jesus is the "author and finisher of our faith" (Heb. 12:2).

The word "author" means creator or originator. When we allow Him to be the author of our natures we are restored to the place where Adam began and that place was one that refreshed and revived us in God's presence. It is the place where we can approach God, we can connect with Him, and we can be near. To be naked is to be in His presence with full assurance and confidence.

When we accept Jesus as Lord and Savior of our lives, we are restored to our positions as sons of God. As a result, we inherit the nature, character, and personality of God and are no longer bound by the Adamic nature. We are given the nature of Christ (see 2 Pet. 1:4). We produce the fruit of Christ's nature in our lives. Our actions become natural to produce the fruit of the Spirit.

Is that the kind of fruit you're producing in your life—love, joy, peace, patience, kindness and so on? If not, who is the author of your nature? Who has been writing on the tablet of your heart?

The apostle Paul confirms our changed status: "Therefore, if anyone is in Christ, he is a new creation; old things have passed away; behold all things have become new" (2 Cor. 5:17). But Paul also makes it clear that we must choose to walk in a manner befitting our changed status.

"You should no longer walk as the rest of the Gentiles walk, in the futility of their mind. Put off, concerning your former conduct, the old man which grows corrupt according to the deceitful lusts, and be renewed in the spirit of your mind, and... put on the new man which was created according to God, in true righteousness and holiness" (Eph. 4:17, 22-24, emphasis added).

Unfortunately, this is not as easy as it sounds. There are so many voices competing for our attention!

Which one are you listening to—God's, the world's, the devil's—or that of your own flesh? What man, what woman, what voice has your undivided attention?

Remember: Whatever you give your attention to determines the nature that rules you. Set your affections on the things of the Kingdom; think on things that are pure, lovely and of good report. (Philippians 4:8)

To walk naked and unashamed is to be clear, to be resolved, to have clarity of your assignment and to be fully confident to approach, to be connected and near to God; to believe His grace is sufficient.

Individual Or Group Study

Meet For A Power Hour Group Study: Invite two other friends to discuss this guide and empower each other as you review this lesson.

Reflections:

1. What does nakedness mean to you?

2. What areas in your life have caused you to remove the mantle of God's covering because you have felt ashamed?

3. Consider your nature deeply, are you producing the fruit of God's nature or that of your own nature.

4. Do you believe that God is still asking the questions of us, where are you and who told you, you were naked?

How has He questioned your whereabouts from His presence?

5. If God's grace is sufficient, how do we avoid being ashamed of our actions?

Prayer: Father, help us to know your voice, our identity and give us the strength of mind to know that you have restored your mantle upon our lives. Teach us to question you when we are questioned. Give us confident assurance that when the enemy comes to accuse us we have a covering that we can lean upon, rest in, be supported, sustained, refreshed and revived. Teach us how to live the Zero life and increase our confidence to approach, remain connected and persist to remain in you.

Memorize WAN Covenant: This covenant is an agreement between a woman and her word, which holds her accountable for her own success. With this joint effort of others, she will achieve it. Embrace these words, live them and act on them. Become all that you are meant to be.

Be A God-Size Dreamer: I am a God-size dreamer, I search my heart, my soul, and my mind to deliver to the world everything I was created to give it.

LESSON SIX
WALK POWERFUL IN GOD'S WORD

The evidence of God's nature will manifest at zero; our experience, more of Him and less of ourselves. Getting to zero develops our strength of mind and empowers our force of behavior to carry out what God's nature would do.

Our struggle remains similar to that of Adam's in that it continues to be a battle of words. The scenes we view and the words we hear create perceptions—that lead to passions—that lead to actions, which develop the habits in our lives. It is by examining these habits that we can determine whose nature is in us. To walk powerful in God's nature means we must walk powerful in His word!

Hearing is especially important in influencing our thoughts. It is one of the most significant ways in which we receive information. In fact, the way we perceive ourselves is based primarily on the words that have been spoken to us.

We should be selective about the words we take into our hearts. What we receive, we believe. What we believe, we become—and act upon. The Bible says, "As [a man] thinks in his heart, so is he" (Prov. 23:7).

Mankind is made of words housed in flesh. We are the words we have received. The enemy has used those closest to us to speak words of curses upon our lives. His goal is to have us not only receive but also speak words that will create a distorted, self-destructive image in our spirits.

God, on the other hand, uses people to speak words of exhortation and encouragement to us. Words fuel the spirit as gasoline fuels an automobile. Our hearts are programmed by words.

Genesis 1 states that "the Spirit of God was hovering over the face of the waters"

(v. 2), waiting for a word from the Lord to go into action. "Then God said, 'Let there be light'; and there was light" (v. 3). Your spirit, too, is waiting for a word from the Lord so that your faith can be made active.

Faith comes by hearing the Word of God. Fear, failure, deceit, confusion and destruction come by hearing the voice of the enemy. Sadly, many Believers have bought into the enemy's lies, accusations and strategies. We have not learned to recognize his devices because we have not spent enough time learning and hearing the Word of God.

The more time we spend in God's Word, the more God's nature will live in us. We will develop a keen awareness of the enemy's devices, and our spirits will be alert and ready to hear the voice of God so that we will "by no means follow a stranger" (John 10:5).

Renewing the Mind

God's plan for our lives is to draw us back to Himself. Sinful habits interrupt this plan by separating us from God. Our habits prevent us from being connected to our Source and focusing on Him so that our nature will be one with His.

But let's face it: Sin is pleasurable. It's enjoyable to the flesh. It satisfies the soul. If we are truly honest with ourselves, we have to admit that we don't want to decrease when faced with difficulty choosing acts of righteousness.

Could this be the reason Paul cried, "I am carnal, sold under sin. For what I am doing, I do not understand. For what I will to do, that I do not practice; but what I hate, that I do"? (Rom. 7:14-15). His flesh and his spirit were at war with one another!

No wonder he advised the Romans, "Therefore, I urge you, brothers, in view of God's mercy, to offer your bodies [the acts of your flesh] as living sacrifices [the sin that is alive in me, that wars against God's Spirit], holy and pleasing to God this [the sacrifice] is your spiritual act of worship" (12:1, NIV, bracketed comments added). He knew that giving up sin was a sacrifice.

A sacrifice requires death. Something must die; something must be killed. Our weapon to destroy the sin that lives in us is our power to make a choice. Choice is the weapon that kills the sacrifice.

We have to choose to fight the war against the flesh. 2 Corinthians 10:4-5 states that "the weapons we fight with are not the weapons of the world. On the contrary, they have divine power to demolish strongholds. We demolish arguments and every pretension that sets itself up against the knowledge of God, and we take captive every thought to make it obedient to Christ."

Thoughts are perceptions put into words. They are what ultimately lead us into sin. The war is in our minds, and we can win the war by being active and alert, ready to demolish every perception that will lead us to ungodly passions and actions. To do this, we must follow Paul's admonition: "Do not conform any longer to the pattern of this world, but be transformed by the renewing of your mind" (Rom. 12:2).

If the enemy can keep us distracted from God's plan, then he will destroy us. That's why it is necessary for us to keep our minds on God and His word. Whatever you give your attention to determines the nature that lives in you.

God has empowered us to win the battle against the enemy. He has "given to us all things that pertain to life and godliness" and has made us "partakers of the divine nature" (2 Pet. 1:3-4, NKJV). We appropriate these things by spending time in His Word—listening to Him—and making a conscious effort to be imitators of Christ so that His nature, and His alone, will empower us to walk naked and unashamed.

Individual Or Group Study

Meet For A Power Hour Group Study: Invite two

other friends to discuss this guide and empower each other as you review this lesson.

Reflections:

1. What have you learned from this lesson that will help you to go deeper still to discover more of God's character?

2. What battle are we constantly fighting? Think about the battlefield of the mind, how do you defeat the voices in your head?

3. Think about a challenge or shortfall you may be experiencing in your life. Write down three new habits you will develop to renew your mind in the word of God.

4. How will you reverse the negative words that have been spoken to you by others?

5. If you are words housed in flesh, what are the most powerful words spoken by God to you that makes you believe He cares about His nature in you?

Prayer: Lord, thank you for helping me to understand that you have given me a divine nature with inherent character that resembles your likeness. Teach me how to understand your Word that I may recognize all things pertaining to life and godliness. I want to be more like you, I want to have thoughts that are driven by your Spirit. Teach me to tame my passions and my desires as I walk powerful with your essence to guide me.

Memorize WAN Covenant:

This covenant is an agreement between a woman and her word, which holds her accountable for her own success. With this joint effort of others, she will achieve it. Embrace these words, live them and act on them. Become all that you are meant to be.

Just Do It - I materialize my thoughts, my ideas, and my dreams!

A Message from the Chief Encouragement Officer, Coach Anna McCoy

Welcome to the seventh and eighth lessons of the Woman Act Now Journey to Zero. Convene with your Power Agents or form a new Power Center of three or more women to experience the journey together.

This study will teach you how to walk powerful successfully and purposefully to fulfill the assignment He has called you to. It will challenge you to question your perspective on both success and purpose while helping you redefine the meaning and benefit of each from God's perspective.

Coach Anna McCoy

LESSON SEVEN
WALK POWERFUL SUCCESSFUL

The psalmist, David, marveled with praise saying, "What a God! His road stretches straight and smooth. Every God-direction is road-tested. Everyone who runs toward him makes it. Is there any god like God? Is not this the God who armed me, then aimed me in the right direction? Now I run like a deer; I'm king of the mountain. He shows me how to fight; I can bend a bronze bow! You protect me with salvation-armor; you hold me up with a firm hand, caress me with your gentle ways. You cleared the ground under me so my footing was firm." Psalms 18:30-35 (The Message Bible.)

I marvel at all that is said about David's journey with God. The pattern of a successful life walking with God is very different than the lessons learned from our culture, authorities, traditions, or educational accomplishment, pursuit, and attainment. To walk powerful in success as one surrendered to God's perspective is directly related to our mental and spiritual core belief. When you face the crises of belief, you must decide what you believe about God.

The core belief I challenge you to question in this lesson is, do you believe the Way of God is perfect? David says, every God-direction is road-tested. Everyone who runs toward him makes it, in other words, He makes my way perfect! If you will decide in this moment that God's ways are perfect and that He will make your way perfect you must helplessly yield your life to walk powerful in His success.

Flawless Perfection

Perfect means conforming absolutely; excellent or complete beyond practical or theoretical improvement; exactly fitting the need in a certain situation or for a certain purpose, entirely without any flaws, defects, or shortcomings; accurate, exact, or correct in every detail.

When we believe that God's WAY is perfect, mentally and spiritually, the opportunity of personal success becomes more concrete, expected and assured. We are not perfect but His Way is perfect, without flaws, or failure. Deciding to live in the WAY we become beneficiaries of success with God. Success by definition changes from a pursuit of man's accolades and financial attainment to that of an empowering ability to consider, to be prudent, circumspect, full of wisdom and understanding to advance or prosper a God-size initiative, thought, idea or assignment.

What blesses me most about this lesson is that success is not what I thought it was, it is not in my doing alone but as I continually pursue God's perfect WAY, not the way I perceive to be right for me but the unfailing, flawless WAY of His word. I am convinced that I am resetting a mental and spiritual success cycle that assures me that as I commit every work to the Lord surely good success will follow.

Living the flawless word in our life allows God to strengthen us and make our way perfect, so much so that He enlarges our path, He keeps our steps steady in the most difficult of circumstances, trains us to hit the mark with accuracy and strength, and prepares and equips us for what is to come. We must keep our eyes always on the LORD. With Him at our right hand, we will be firm, focused and faithful to walk in the perfect WAY of the Lord.

Divine success is the result of the mindset of obedience rather than the pursuit of our own sensible and temporal desires. It's much easier than we think and success is guaranteed. We are God's assignment and He assigns our portion daily, His cup He has given is sufficient (Psalm 16:5), and what is inside of that cup remains the same with every drink, "be it unto me according to thy Word, or may it be just as you said." To be effective in your assigned moment your response after every drink of the cup must become "yes, Lord, I am willing," that is the greatest attribute of the Zero life that walks powerful in success.

With every yielded response of "I am willing," an adjustment in your life will be expected. It is impossible to do what you want to do and do what God wants you to do at the same time. Most of us want to continue our agendas, continue in our lifestyle of moral excellence rather than spiritual success manifesting God's ways and fulfilling His purposes. When God speaks to you, revealing what He is about to do, that revelation is your invitation to adjust your life to Him.

Once you have adjusted your life to Him, His purposes, and His ways, you are in a position to obey. In every recorded biblical experience of a person walking with God had to make an adjustment in their life to obey God before they took action. Noah could not continue life as usual and build an ark at the same time (Genesis 6). Moses could not stay on the back side of the desert herding sheep and stand before Pharaoh at the same time (Exodus 3). Peter, Andrew, James and John had to leave their fishing business in order to follow Jesus (Matthew 4:18-22). My adjustment; stay in my comfort zone of home and family or travel globally to encourage the women of the world to achieve their God-given destiny. What adjustment is required of you? You may be called to attempt things that only God can do, where formerly you may have attempted only that which you knew you could do. Are you willing to accept God-size assignments to walk powerful successfully with God?

Individual Or Group Study
Meet For A Power Hour Group Study: Invite two

other friends to discuss this guide and empower each other as you review this lesson.

Reflections:

1. What does God want you to do in response to what you have learned in this lesson?

2. What belief crisis have you been faced with that made you question what you believe about God?

3. What have you discovered about success and its relationship to God's ability to make your way perfect?

4. Think about the last thing you really believe God instructed you to do, what prevented you from obeying Him?

5. How will you apply walking powerful successfully in your life now? List any adjustments that you may have to make to get in step with God's will.

Prayer: Father, I need to walk in your path, I need to believe your Way is perfect for me. Help me to trust you, to believe you have plans and hopes for me far greater than I can hope for myself. Teach me to trust what you tell me, teach me to believe what you say to me. When I hear you help me to shift and adjust my life to obey you with actions that please you. I want to be your success story, not one that I create. Lord, I am willing. In Jesus Name.

Memorize WAN Covenant: This covenant is an agreement between a woman and her word, which holds her accountable for her own success. With this joint effort of others, she will achieve it. Embrace these words, live them and act on them. Become all that you are meant to be.

Give More Than Required: I give more than required and value relationships with other like-minded individuals.

LESSON EIGHT
WALK POWERFUL PURPOSEFUL

Most of us are baffled by the questions, why am I here, who am I and what does God want me to do? I too, through much prayer sought answers and the power-purpose-success cycle was God's gift I can offer you to help you define and pursue your God-given destiny. This defined cycle has helped me to gain tremendous peace, clarity, and direction in my journey of understanding why I am here and how to live life on purpose.

Prayer

Prayer is a means of having a relationship with God. It is the instruction we receive and communication we have with our Maker. Prayer involves us presenting our heavenly Father with requests and petitions, and it offers us the comfort of developing intimacy with Him. Prayer is the place for transformation personally and socially.

Prayer helps us to think deeply and with greater clarity about who we are and what we do. It helps us to meditate, listen and separate ourselves from the noise and clutter of our daily lives in order to enjoy peace in our souls.

Prayer helps us to learn how to get to ZERO so that our self-absorbed egos diminish while at the same time increasing our estimation and appreciation of God's greatness. By praying, we learn to be humble as we seek God for information we admit we do not know; we request help for ourselves and others. Prayer is a safe place to experience, learn, touch, hear and develop the I AM in our personal self. Prayer builds confidence to live, thrive and to be!

In Luke 9:29, "as he was praying, the appearance of his face changed (became different) and his clothes became as bright as a flash of lightning. Prayer is essential to knowing the will of God. It is transformative and revealing. Jesus had an encounter with Moses and Elijah who told him of His departure. Prayer confirms your identity in God. (Luke 9:35) Prayer changes you, it re-orients your life to God, and it focuses your life on God's purpose and not on your own plans. It causes you to seek to see from God's perspective rather than from your own frail human perspective. Prayer recalibrates our location with God; it is our God Positioning System. Ultimately prayer equips us to walk successfully in the perfect Way of God.

Passion

Passion is an internal drive that is stimulated by forces that are positive and negative, external and internal. In order to be effective, passions must be intentional. Unbridled passion is destructive; with too much power and too little direction, it causes any plans or pursuits to derail. God is intentional, and when we allow Him to direct our passions and strong emotions, passion becomes the productive ingredient to achieving what we intend to. Passion often breeds obsession, which is good only if directed toward the right targets, and to a healthy degree. An obsession dominates one's thoughts or feelings; it is usually a persistent idea, image, or desire. Passion breeds determination, distinction, and directions, all of which are essential for production and success.

Persistence

Doing what God tells you to do over and over — continuing in spite of opposition and persecution—means that you recognize resistance as a sign to encourage you to move forward. To persist as zero is to do whatever is necessary to abide, stay or remain in God (revisit lesson 3 Walk Powerful to Persist).

Persistence is similar to perseverance, a quality that the author of Hebrews encouraged believers to exhibit: "Let us throw off everything that hinders and the sin that so easily entangles, and let us run with perseverance the race marked out for us" (Hebrews 12:1 NIV). Also, Jesus told His disciples, "Ask and it will be given to you; seek and you will find; knock and door will be opened to you" (Matthew 7:7 NIV)

Purpose Defined

These four thoughts helped me to write a personal definition of the word purpose.

1. Godly instruction I hear when I pray.
2. Fulfilled intentions.
3. Reason for existence.
4. Purpose is not tangible it is movement, direction.

Purpose: Desire of mind and heart directed for the fulfillment of Godly instruction. The definition encompasses prayer represented by godly instruction; passion, represented by desire; persistence, represented by the act of directing mind and heart; and purpose itself represented by fulfillment. No longer do you have to see to accomplish or to be; fulfill the instruction you receive through prayer and meditation with God.

As you do this, rely on Him, and your former frustration with trying to discern God's purpose will be transformed into a joyful journey of seeking Him for instruction and purpose.

Based on this new understanding of the word purpose your responsibility becomes directing your passions and when you hear or know what you are to do, believe God and persist until you get it done. If you succeed in following the instructions, you are living your life on purpose. You are well able to walk powerful purposefully.

Individual Or Group Study

Meet For A Power Hour Group Study: Invite two

other friends to discuss this guide and empower each other as you review this lesson.

Reflections:

1. How effective do you believe your prayer life is?

2. When you receive instruction in the place of prayer do you persist, believe God until you get it done?

3. What are you passionate about? Are you intentional about it?

4. How do you respond when you encounter resistance while fulfilling God's instructions?

5. Now that you know that purpose is movement not necessarily a destination what adjustments will you make in your life in order to fulfill your God-ordained purpose?

Prayer: Father, I thank you for the revelation of knowing that my purpose is not farfetched. Help me Lord, to persist to seek your face in prayer that I may direct my passions, receive instructions and follow them by your leading and thereby live my life on purpose. I want to give it all it takes and live by your definition of success no matter the opposition I face. In Jesus name.

Memorize WAN Covenant: This covenant is an agreement between a woman and her word, which holds her accountable for her own success. With this joint effort of others, she will achieve it. Embrace these words, live them and act on them. Become all that you are meant to be.

 Intentional Integrity: I demonstrate character, integrity, and leadership in the marketplace.

A Message from the Chief Encouragement Officer, Coach Anna McCoy

Welcome to the ninth and tenth lesson of the Woman Act Now Journey to Zero. Convene with your Power Agents or form a new Power Center of three or more women to experience the journey together.

This study will teach you how to walk powerful in mercy and love to release grace, true justice, and forgiveness that will cause others to glorify God's goodness. You will be challenged and equipped to trust that Jesus paid the price once for all and become the carrier of Christ's love as the mercy seat for others to run to as they experience unfailing love through you.

LESSON NINE
WALK POWERFUL IN MERCY

Mercy creates an atmosphere for God's original intention to be restored in a situation whether deserving or undeserving. In the scriptures, Jesus is confronted by the Pharisees about what is lawful on the Sabbath. He establishes a truth about Himself by saying, "I tell you that one greater than the temple is here. If you had known what these words mean, I desire mercy, not sacrifice; you would not have condemned the innocent. For the Son of

Man is the Lord of the Sabbath."

Going on from that place, He went into their synagogue, and a man with a shriveled hand was there. Looking for a reason to accuse Jesus, they asked Him, "Is it lawful to heal on the Sabbath?" He said to them. If any of you has a sheep and it falls into a pit on the Sabbath, will you not take hold of it and lift it out? How much more valuable is a man than a sheep! Therefore, it is lawful to do good on the Sabbath. Then He said to the man, "Stretch out your hand." So he stretched it out and it was completely restored, just as sound as the other. (Matthew 12:6-14) Jesus demonstrated mercy and compassion, "This was to fulfill what was spoken through the prophet Isaiah. "Here is my servant whom I have chosen, the one I love, in whom I delight; I will put my Spirit on him, and he will proclaim justice to the nations." (Matthew 12:17-18).

And the word of the Lord came again to Zechariah: "This is what the Lord Almighty says: 'Administer true justice; show mercy and compassion to one another.' Do not oppress the widow or the fatherless, the alien or the poor. In your hearts do not think evil of each other." (Zechariah 7:9, NIV)

Let me explain. What distracts us from walking in the power of the resurrection in our lives is the belief that we have a right to withhold forgiveness because of offenses against us. There is a greater law at work as a believer; Jesus has already paid the price for our sin.

Through mercy, we can give a gift to others and restore what God would intend for the outcome in that situation. Mercy is God's unfailing love; it is His restoration of the infallible, indestructible intention of His heart. His mercy endures forever and is renewed every morning. Mercy takes you deeper still to understand more of Christ's nature. "For I desire mercy, not sacrifice, and acknowledgment of God rather than burnt offering." (Hosea 6:6 NIV)

If mercy is God's unfailing love and He desires that we show mercy to each other, He is really asking us to do to others as we would have them do to us. You might say, "God has the power to extend mercy but it is impossible for me." It is possible...I pray that out of His glorious riches He may strengthen you with power through His Spirit in your inner being so that Christ may dwell in your heart through faith. And I pray that you, being rooted and established in love, may have power, together with all the saints, to grasp how wide and long and high and deep is the love of Christ and to know this love that surpasses knowledge—that you may be filled to the measure of all the fullness of God (Ephesians 3:16-19 NIV)

Christ The Mercy Seat

If Christ dwells in you, you have the enabling presence of God to allow mercy to function through you. The tabernacle in the wilderness required yearly sacrifices for the remission of sins and the sprinkling of blood on the mercy seat by the High Priest on behalf of the people. We are like that tabernacle; the House of God, moving and having our being in Him and He in us. The mercy seat is Jesus Christ and He lives in us. We extend mercy and restore hope, forgiveness, and healing to others. Love is defined as contending for the highest possible good to be manifested in the present moment. Compassion overrides the emotions or circumstances and expresses tender affection towards others. For those who cried out "Son of

David, have mercy on me in Matthew 9, they may have said this differently if they were saying it to us. "Consider me as yourself, would you not contend for my highest good to manifest? My actions may have warranted my condition or perhaps I was born this way but treat me as your brother. Have compassion for me, deliver me, heal me, free me from my oppression. Let your tender love and kindness give me grace instead of what I am due." When Jesus hears this cry as the mercy seat dwelling in you, His love will arise and say, "Your sins are forgiven, be healed, be whole, be complete."

Mercy Always Wins

• The power of God's mercy is revealed in those who walk before Him in truth, in righteousness, and in uprightness of heart.

• Mercy sees redemption the way God sees. Have mercy despite what you think is deserved.

• Where mercy and truth collide, righteousness and peace have kissed. Psalms 85:10

• Mercy perfects that which concerns you. God does not abandon the work of His hands regardless of its condition. Mercy allows Him to return to it again and again. Psalms 138:8

• Mercy quenches anger and restores love to any situation.

• The zero life is a life of mercy and truth. The truth of knowing you are nothing and the yielding of being right when you deal with others who have offended you, let mercy reign.

• Mercy causes you to go deeper still beyond the outer court, through the chatter of the inner court to the mercy seat of God's perspective. Upon experiencing His perspective, you discern and extend compassion so great that His loving kindness through you is experienced by the receiver as an extension of His mercy as His glory is revealed and celebrated beyond your own doing!

Group or Individual Study

Meet For A Power Hour Group Study: Invite two other friends to discuss this guide and empower each other as you review this lesson.

Reflections:

1. How does this lesson inspire you to extend mercy to others?

2. What have you learned about how you have demonstrated mercy toward others?

3. Should mercy be given in every situation? If not, when should it be withheld?

4. Think of a situation you may be involved in now in which you have not forgiven someone, how will you apply mercy to the situation?

5. What is the ultimate aim of mercy in God's eyes?

Prayer: Father, give me a heart of understanding to consider others as myself. Teach me how to allow Jesus to be experienced through me and to extend mercy and not hinder them because of my judgment. Teach me how to love like you and restore others as you have restored me. Empower me with your presence to be merciful and compassionate. In Jesus Name.

Memorize WAN Covenant: This covenant is an agreement between a woman and her word, which holds her accountable for her own success. With this joint effort of others, she will achieve it. Embrace these words, live them and act on them. Become all that you are meant to be.

Excellent In Spirit: I am a woman of an excellent spirit, it is my right and my essence and I seek improvement continuously.

LESSON TEN
WALK POWERFUL IN WISDOM

"If any of you lacks wisdom, he should ask God, who gives generously to all without finding fault, and it will be given to him."(James 1:5, NIV).

This lesson has the potential to change your approach to how you view lack. Rather than seeing it as a negative change see it as a way of empowering you to ask for wisdom in the area you have insufficiency.

The word "lack" is the Greek word leipo

(pronounced lie-po), a word that conveys a deficit of some kind. To be deficient is to not have enough, having a shortfall, or scarcity.

Although we might experience pain and suffering when we don't have enough to pay our bills, fix a broken relationship or turn our business around, a "lack" of "wisdom" is the most devastating kind of deficit a person can face. Wisdom delivers answers and gives solutions needed to turn any situation around for the better. We are at a great disadvantage when we are bereft of wisdom; we are nearly paralyzed because we don't know what to do!

In James 1:5 the word "wisdom" is the Greek word sophias. This word sophias could describe enlightenment or even special insight. It also means to have wisdom that is broad and full of intelligence; or knowledge of very diverse matters. The wisdom which belongs to men is the varied knowledge of things human and divine, acquired by acuteness (keen perception or discernment) and experience, and summed up in maxims (rules of conduct) and proverbs (basic truth or practical precept).

Do you need wisdom for a particular situation? Have answers evaded you no matter how hard you tried? If so, it's time to get a good dose of wisdom from on High! James says, "If any of you lack wisdom, let him ask of God...."

The word "ask" is the Greek word aiteo (pronounced i-te-o). The word aiteo expresses the idea that the one asking has a full expectation to receive what has been firmly requested.

In this verse, to "ask" God for wisdom in the Greek tense is referred to as a command.

This plainly means God isn't suggesting that we come to

Him for wisdom; He is commanding us to do so!

"When these words are used together in one phrase, it could be translated:

"If anyone lacks insight, let him firmly request it..." "If anyone has a shortage of wisdom, he should demand it..." "If anyone is baffled and doesn't know what to do, he should be bold to ask..." Rick Renner, Sparkling Gems.

Rather than continue to struggle, why don't you ask God to give you the necessary wisdom to conquer the situation you are facing right now? You have every right to ask Him. In fact, God commands you to come to Him when you lack wisdom! So take a few minutes today, ask God to give you strength to seek His wisdom today. You have the power to ask Him for access to His wisdom chamber and sit with Him at the counsel table.

Solomon Asked For Wisdom

"Give me wisdom and knowledge, that I may lead this people, for who is able to govern this great people of yours?" God said to Solomon, "Since this is your heart's desire and you have not asked for wealth, riches or honor, nor for the death of your enemies, and since you have not asked for a long life but for wisdom and knowledge to govern my people over whom I have made you king, therefore wisdom and knowledge will be given you. And I will also give you wealth, riches and honor, such as no king who was before you ever had and none after you will have." (2 Chronicles 1:10–12 NIV)

When a person lacks wisdom he can ask God and He will give it to him liberally. God knows everything. Wisdom cannot exist without a knowledge of all the facts pertinent to any purpose or plan. Theologians use the term "omniscient" when speaking of God's infinite knowledge. God knows everything about everything. He knows what men are thinking (see Ezekiel 11:5; Luke 5:21-22). He knows everything that is going to happen. He even knows everything that could happen, under any set of circumstances (1 Samuel 23:10-12; 2 Kings 8:10). God cannot devise a bad plan or fail to bring His purposes to their conclusion because He knows everything. His omniscience undergirds His wisdom.

Wisdom is not just knowledge, but "know how." God's wisdom enables Him to "know how" to do anything (see 2 Peter 2:9). Wisdom entails the skillfulness to formulate a plan and use the best means for execution. Bezalel was a craftsman, a man with incredible "wisdom" in the art of making the furnishings for the Tabernacle (Exodus 31:1-5). Joshua had been given wisdom to know how to lead Israel (Deuteronomy 34:9). Solomon asked for and received the wisdom and knowledge needed to rule Israel (2 Chronicles 1:7-12).

Attaining wisdom is the result of asking and walking with God. Wisdom:
• is a supernatural skill to accomplish something you know little about
• is shrewdness (characterized by keen awareness, sharp intelligence)
• is prudence (refer to the exercise of good judgment, common sense, and even caution)
• is unashamedly ethical (accepted principles of right and wrong)
• seeks to hear God and increases learning
• understands the fear of God

• is insight and comprehension
• has quick and correct perceptions
• is discreet (wise self-restraint in speech and behavior)
• is circumspect (heedful of potential consequences)

"Wisdom is the power to see, and the inclination to choose, the best and highest goal, together with the surest means of attaining it. Wisdom is, in fact, the practical side of moral goodness. As such, it is found in its fullness only in God. He alone is naturally and entirely and invariably wise." J. I. Packer

Individual Or Group Study

Invite two or three of your friends to discuss and empower each other as you review this lesson.

Reflections:

1. How have you viewed lack in your life? Describe whether it was positive or negative?

2. How do you invite wisdom in your daily life to be your guide to achieving your dreams?

3. Think of a time when you couldn't figure something out and you asked for wisdom, how did God answer you?

4. What are you most afraid of asking God's wisdom on? What keeps you from asking Him now?

Prayer: Lord, help me to come to You when I find myself lacking answers. When I have done all I know to do, remind me that every answer I need you have. Your wisdom holds the answers I am looking for; therefore, I am making the decision to ask often! Give me the confidence that I fully hear your voice and I can walk in the steps you have ordered for me to solve the problem I face today. I pray this in Jesus' name!

Memorize WAN Covenant: This covenant is an agreement between a woman and her word, which holds her accountable for her own success. With this joint effort of others, she will achieve it. Embrace these words, live them and act on them. Become all that you are meant to be.

Woman Of My Word: I am a woman of my word. I am intentional with actions and I keep my commitments to myself, family and community.

A Message from the Chief Encouragement Officer, Coach Anna McCoy

Welcome to the eleventh and twelfth lessons of the Woman Act Now Journey to Zero. Convene with your Power Agents or form a new Power Center of three or more women to experience the journey together.

This study will teach you how to walk powerful, broken open by your own will to release the potential of your greatness within you. You will learn five lessons that the breaking releases when your heart opens to receive God's word. When the outer man is broken the heart is now ready to obey as a "sent one" to do the will of God.

Coach Anna McCoy

LESSON ELEVEN
WALK POWERFUL OPEN BROKEN

What do the seed and the rosebud have in common with the inward man of the heart? Each must break from the inside out to release the potential that the Creator put in them.

The Lord Jesus tells us in John 12:24,"Except the grain of wheat falling into the ground dies, it abides alone; but if it dies, it bears much fruit." Life is in the grain of wheat, but the outer shell must be broken for life to grow and multiply. As long as the shell of the seed is not open broken, from the inside out, the wheat cannot grow, mature or reproduce. When the earth is not broken to yield moisture it cannot provide the right atmosphere or condition for the seed to take root within it.

The heart of man is symbolic of the soil of the earth and the soil is as important to the maturation of the seed as the seed is to the soil. The soil has no purpose without the seed planted within it. Both must be broken to release their greatness within.

The Seed

"You have been born anew, not from perishable seed, but from imperishable seed, through the living and enduring word of God," 1 Peter 1:23. The parable of the sower speaks of a sower who went out to sow his seed. And as he sowed, some fell along the path and was trampled on, and wild birds devoured them, others fell on rocks and withered because they had no moisture. Other seeds fell among the thorns, and the thorns grew with them and choked them. But other seeds fell on good soil and grew, and it produced a hundred times as much grain. As Jesus said this, he called out, "The one who has ears to hear had better listen!" Luke 8:11 states, now the parable means this: The seed is the word of God. Luke 8:14. As for the seed that fell among thorns, these are the ones who hear, but as they go on their way they are choked by the worries and riches and pleasures of life, and their fruit does not mature. Luke 8:15. But as for the seed that landed on good soil, these are the ones who after hearing the word, cling to it with an honest and good heart, and bear fruit with steadfast endurance.

The Breaking Releases

Anyone who hears the word of the Kingdom and does not understand it, the wicked one comes to catch away what was sown in his heart. When the heart does not understand it is like the word falling by the wayside to be consumed so that the receiver will not experience the benefit of maturity, fruitfulness and productivity.

How Do We Break Open With Steadfast Endurance?

1. Develop the habit of "use". The habit of "use" is the practice of cultivating your heart to receive the word of God and being available for His use. It is making your field ready to receive the instruction of the Lord. It is learning how to pay attention to the voice of God so that you will do what He tells you to do. The breaking releases a willingness in your heart to be used of the Lord in your daily life.

2. Practice surrendered obedience. The heart that is nurtured and ready to receive the seed of God's word yields and submits immediately at the initial prompting of the recognized voice of God. It doesn't question because it has developed an involuntary response to doing what God says. It no longer allows its will to be its master but acts quickly in response to God's instructions and follows Him wholeheartedly.

3. Practice His presence. Become the host of God's presence. Welcome the presence of God always in your life. There is no place to escape His presence, yield to knowing that He is omniscient and omnipresent.

4. Give your everyday life to God. Romans 12:1, 2 (The

Message) So here's what I want you to do, God helping you; Take your everyday, ordinary life—your sleeping, eating, going-to-work, and walking-around-life—and place it before God as an offering. Embracing what God does for you is the best thing you can do for him. Don't become so well-adjusted to your culture that you fit into it without even thinking. Instead, fix your attention on God. You'll be changed from the inside out. Readily recognize what he wants from you, and quickly respond to it. Unlike the culture around you, always dragging you down to its level of immaturity, God brings the best out of you, develops well-formed maturity in you."

5. The eye must be single. "The lamp of the body is the eye." Matthew 6:22. The light of the heart is God's word. The lamp of the body is the eye which reflects the light of God's word. Light relates to God, the lamp, the illumination or reflection of the light relates to man. The lamp is the place where light is retained. The lamp is the place where God deposits His light. It is also the place where we retain and release the light of Christ. In order for God's word to shine in us, we must have a lamp within us. This lamp is our eye. "If therefore your eye is single, your whole body will be full of light; but if your eye is evil, your whole body will be dark." In order for your whole body to be full of light, the Lord specified one condition—the eye must be single. We must serve God; it is impossible to serve two masters. Choosing God completely opens our eye to radiate with the light of Christ from within.

Like the Rose

"When we plant a rose seed in the earth, we notice it is small, but we do not criticize it as "rootless and stemless." We treat it as a seed, giving it the water and nourishment required of a seed. When it first shoots up out of the earth, we don't condemn it as immature and underdeveloped, nor do we criticize the buds for not being open when they appear. We stand in wonder at the process taking place and give the plant the care it needs at each stage of its development.

The rose is a rose from the time it is a seed to the time it dies. Within it, at all times, it contains its whole potential. It seems to be constantly in the process of change: yet at each state, at each moment, it is perfectly all right as it is.

"A flower is not better when it blooms than when it is merely a bud; at each stage, it is the same thing — a flower in the process of expressing its potential." W. Timothy Gallway

So is the human heart and the inward man; our growth is an expression of our potential within. Allow the breaking to occur from within.

Individual Or Group Study

Meet For A Power Hour Group Study: Invite two other friends to discuss this guide and empower each other as you review this lesson.

Reflections:

1.   Read Matthew 13:18 and measure the condition of your heart. Is your heart open broken like good soil to receive the word of God?

2.   What do you find to be most difficult when you hear God's instruction?

3.   Have you ever found yourself wanting to do

something that you know you should do but your outer man will not allow you to do it? Describe a situation where your flesh did not break and obey.

4. What is the difference between surrendered obedience and obeying God?

5. What does it mean to give your everyday life to God?

Prayer: Father, teach me how to surrender my life to you in such a way that I am willing to obey you at any cost. Many times I hear you but I just can't carry out your commands and I need your help. I yield my heart as soil for you to plant the seed of your word in me. I will cling to it and allow you to nurture it to bring forth fruit in my life. In Jesus Name.

Memorize WAN Covenant: This covenant is an agreement between a woman and her word, which holds her accountable for her own success. With this joint effort of others, she will achieve it. Embrace these words, live them and act on them. Become all that you are meant to be.

Willing In Spirit: I am a woman wholly devoted to hearing and obeying the word in my life, yielding my will to follow the instruction of the Lord in my life.

LESSON TWELVE
WALK POWERFUL SENT

Welcome to the twelfth lesson in our study on how to journey into Zero. It is my prayer that this journey has been as transformative and informative for you as it has been for us. Seeing that it is the last lesson in this volume, we want to bring together everything that we have learned so far. Even though we might not have been very clear in the beginning where this was all headed, it is wonderful to see how the Holy Spirit has led us to the place where the

Purpose for this journey is now revealed!

It was all so that we may ARISE and take our place amongst the sent! That is why we are closing with nuggets on how to Walk Powerful Sent.

The breaking of the outer man releases the potential within us. When we are broken we are now ready to be used of God and sent forth to do what He tells us to do as "sent ones."

The Sent Ones – are the answer! Woman, we hope this journey to Walk Powerful as Zero is equipping you to be more effective in your daily walk with God to fulfill what you hear the Father say. These twelve affirmations are a reminder of the investment you have made for yourselves, your friends, and your effort during the past twelve lessons.

1. Spirit: I AM sent with a surrendered, obedient and radical spirit to soar above my own limitations.

2. Vision: I AM sent possessing an amazingly clear vision that is focused on a steadfast hope in the future God has planned for me.

3. Persist: I AM sent with a heart strengthened to persist to remain and abide completely with Him no matter the difficulty.

4. Being: I AM sent as a host of His Ever present presence, empowering me to live, move and have my being in Him.

5. Naked and unashamed: I AM sent as a new (wo)man who was created according to God, in true righteousness and holiness and I walk with Him naked and unashamed.

6. God's Word: I AM sent by His authored and finished Word. My requirement: hear it, see it, do it, NOW!

7. Success: I AM sent in His perfect WAY, committing every work to Him; I achieve success without flaws or failure!

8. Purpose: I AM sent with a desire of mind and heart directed for the fulfillment of Godly instruction enabling me to live my life on purpose.

9. Mercy: I AM sent to live a life of mercy and truth, the truth of knowing I am everything with Him; I choose forgiveness and mercy always wins.

10. Wisdom: I AM sent with wisdom to deliver significant answers and execute principles to reverse any situation for the highest good.

11. Open Broken: I AM sent open broken with a heart cultivated to receive His Word and be available for His immediate use.

12. Sent: I am a "sent one" on assignment to execute my life to the highest level of obedience to God as a disciple of Jesus to share the good news and transfer the spirit of faith to the next generation of kingdom citizens to advance, accomplish, execute and finish well.

The Kingdom Of Heaven Is Near!

Matthew 10 states, "As we GO, plead this cause: The Kingdom of Heaven is near! When the sent one knows the "I AM," the Ever present presence is within them, we go with the "I AM," the kingdom of heaven (all power and authority of the "I AM") and we bring the Kingdom of Heaven near to the dry, lifeless places. We heal the sick; raise the dead, cast out demons! The kingdom of heaven is within us and when we enter an atmosphere we proclaim the language of the Kingdom of Heaven and activate the benefits upon the earth."

Walk powerful. As God sends you forward you will have the entire support of eternity itself undergirding you to complete what God has sent you to do. You are not alone!

The Father seeks such to worship Him...

Who is this woman that God seeks to worship Him?

Who is this woman that can be found grounded in truth?

For she is the one the Father seeks.

Who is this woman that resonates with the presence of God?

For this is the woman the Father seeks.

She is the woman that will worship Him in spirit and in truth!

When the Ever present presence of God fills your being you will be found by God, for the Father seeks such to worship Him and sends that one to do His will!

Go. Arise and walk powerful as a "sent one." We are the generation to be found by God.

Individual Or Group Study

Meet For A Power Hour Group Study: Invite two other friends to discuss this guide and empower each other as you review this lesson.

Reflections:

1. How will you ready yourself daily to be sent by God at any given moment?

2. Review the affirmations above, which of these resonate with where you are in your walk with God?

3. Develop the practice of being available as a "sent one." Write or print out each affirmation on a sheet of paper or

index card and purpose in your heart that day to be awakened to that principle. At the end of the day measure your progress, how did you do? Continue doing this simple exercise until you have developed the habit of "use" with that affirmation.

4. As a group, you can participate together by touching base with each other at the end of the day or week to measure your growth and be accountable to each other.

Prayer: Woman Act Now Charge as "Sent Ones"

Father, we declare: We are women who are transformed by the renewing of our mind. We are women who hold the heart of God, we contend for the highest possible good to be manifested in the present moment. We are women with an excellent spirit, women who are being made more excellent by you, Father. We are women of royalty; we are the King's girls with rights and privileges of the Kingdom of God and Heaven.

We have benefits unseen. Teach us the language of the King, teach us how to negotiate, how to command and decree and create policies and laws on behalf of the King of Kings. Father, we thank you that we are women who house the glorious riches of God. The fruit of your Spirit is rich within us. We are women of a disciplined spirit, masters of our emotions, we simmer, we get to zero, we decrease for you to arise and help us do your will. We are women of action, we are servants of the most high we give our lives in surrender, send us, we will go! Amen.

Memorize Wan Covenant: This covenant is an agreement between a woman and her word, which holds her accountable for her own success. With this joint effort of others, she will achieve it. Embrace these words, live them and act on them. Become all that you are meant to be.

Trust: I am a woman who believes you are my Father and Lord of my life, you are for me and I will trust you completely.

Thank you for taking the journey of zero and creating a powerful walk with God.
Please share your comments on Facebook.

Please connect with us on:
Twitter @womanactnow, @coachannamccoy
facebook.com/womanactnow
facebook.com/coachannamccoy
Instagram: coachanna
Linkedin:www.linkedin.com/in/annamccoy

For more information on training or coaching with Anna McCoy visit www.equiplounge.com or annamccoy.com

To purchase a copy of Woman Act Now, The Book visit www.annamccoy.com or visit the kindle store at amazon.com.

To order your One Woman One Girl Confidence Bracelet visit www.annamccoy.com

If you have enjoyed this study, please provide a review to encourage others to take the journey also at www.bit.ly/walkzero

We invite you to visit our website at www.annamccoy.com and find out more about how to work with Coach Anna McCoy and Arise into your Greatness.

Below is the purpose statement for the One Woman One Girl bracelet you may purchase. This bracelet is inspired by the Holy Spirit as a testament to the brilliance within you as a woman of destiny and purpose. Memorize each of the jewel meanings. Like many of the women who have purchased and received this bracelet, it becomes a favorite and valuable item.

If you follow me on Facebook you will see this bracelet in many of my pictures as I travel the world empowering women. I wear it daily so that I can give it to a woman as the Lord leads me. I have given hundreds away since I created it in 2012. I hope you too will be encouraged as I and others have been. Also, let it be a reminder of who the "I AM" is in you and share it with others.

Women are just amazing and I just love it when a woman's motive moves her heart so compellingly that she impacts multitudes with her dream. Be that Woman! You are joining women from 5 continents who wear this bracelet as a reminder to Arise into Greatness and transfer their wisdom to the next generation to start the cycle all over again.

Bracelet Meaning

This is the meaning of the bracelet and I hope you will be inspired to learn its meaning and use the bracelet to encourage one woman a week to arise into her greatness. Coach Anna has personally given hundreds of these bracelets to women on the plane, in restaurants, or business meetings. Your purchase allows us to make 3 more bracelets to give to women in other nations to encourage them to Arise!

One Woman: I am a woman of an Industrious Spirit, I am an advancer, accomplisher, executor, and finisher.

Wings: I S.O.A.R. I am Surrendered, Obedient and Radical. (I must yield to soar as an eagle and let the wind of God's spirit take me where He wants me to go).

Key: I have an assignment to accomplish my Kingdom mandate and my purpose in life, I hold the key to my destiny!

Butterfly: I am transformed by the renewing of my mind as I evolve into my infinite greatness. What is in me you can't always see on the surface but I am emerging as an incredible woman of God.

Heart: I have God's heart of love - I contend for the highest possible good to be manifested until it is a present tense reality.

Blue Stone: I am a woman of an excellent spirit, forever seeking peace and truth. I serve an excellent God and excellence is my birth right and I demonstrate excellence in every area of my life.

Purple Stone: I am royalty, I speak the language of the Kingdom of Heaven. As it is in Heaven so shall it be on earth. The words I speak are life and prosperity (meaning to flourish, succeed, thrive, and prosper with ease and flow.)

Orange Stone: I am a wealthy woman, I am full of wisdom, knowledge and the glorious riches of God. I am a virtuous (Chayil in Hebrew) woman and I manifest faith, wisdom, strength, honor, worship, favor, and influence.

Red Stone: I am a woman of action, confidence, courage, and vitality. I am an overcomer by the word of my testimony and the blood of the Lamb. I am resilient, I practice bouncing back and overcoming. For Greater is He that is in me than the evil in the world!

Braided Circles: Represents a Power Center - Three

women coming together as circles of influence for accountability, stability, and reliability. A three braided cord is not easily broken, it is collaboration, confluence, and connection.

Jewel: I am committed to transferring jewels of wisdom and the purposes of God to the next generation of Kingdom citizens to start the cycle over again.

Knot: The knot is tied 8 times as a reminder you can begin again. The biblical meaning of the number 8 is "new beginnings." Woman, it's not over until it is over and if you can still breathe… believe you can begin again.

Boot: This boot is only on bracelets that women receive when they come for a personal training intensive with Coach Anna McCoy and her team held at the Equip Lounge in Arlington, TX, as a Texas memento.

Get Involved and Learn, Teach, Give

Become a Confidence Trainer: Be sure to check annamccoy.com for videos and curriculum that compliments the teachings on the bracelet. Check upcoming events at http://www.equiplounge.com

Individual Purchases: http://www.annamccoy.com
Group Purchases: You can order the bracelets for groups and string them together as you teach your women and girls how to build confidence, connect with each other and collaborate.

Fundraising: In addition you can also participate in helping us to empower girls of the world to be more confident by fundraising and selling the bracelets. You will assist us in giving 3 bracelets and 3 reusable menstrual pads to girls in Uganda, South Africa and Nigeria giving them an opportunity to stay in school and learn confidence through the principles of the bracelet.

Sponsorships: If you would like to partner with us please call 877.751.5700 x 401 for more information. Sponsorships, alliances, and partners are welcome.

Be blessed and be that woman who will be the change in her world.

Coach Anna McCoy

NOTES – Lesson 1

Lesson 2

_____
_____
_____
_____
_____
_____
_____
_____
_____
_____
_____
_____
_____
_____
_____
_____
_____
_____
_____
_____
_____
_____
_____
_____
_____
_____
_____
_____

Lesson 3

_____
_____
_____
_____
_____
_____
_____
_____
_____
_____
_____
_____
_____
_____
_____
_____
_____
_____
_____
_____
_____
_____
_____
_____
_____
_____
_____

Lesson 4

Lesson 5

_____
_____
_____
_____
_____
_____
_____
_____
_____
_____
_____
_____
_____
_____
_____
_____
_____
_____
_____
_____
_____
_____
_____
_____
_____
_____
_____

Lesson 6

_____
_____
_____
_____
_____
_____
_____
_____
_____
_____
_____
_____
_____
_____
_____
_____
_____
_____
_____
_____
_____
_____
_____
_____
_____
_____
_____
_____
_____
_____

Lesson 7

Lesson 8

Lesson 9

_____

_____

_____

_____

_____

_____

_____

_____

_____

_____

_____

_____

_____

_____

_____

_____

_____

_____

_____

_____

_____

_____

_____

_____

_____

_____

_____

Lesson 10

_____
_____
_____
_____
_____
_____
_____
_____
_____
_____
_____
_____
_____
_____
_____
_____
_____
_____
_____
_____
_____
_____
_____
_____
_____
_____
_____

Lesson 11

Lesson 12

Coach Anna McCoy

35604688R00061

Made in the USA
San Bernardino, CA
29 June 2016